easy french
cooking

CAROL COLBERT

THE CROSSING PRESS
FREEDOM, CALIFORNIA

For information on bulk purchases or group discounts for this and
other Crossing Press titles, please contact our Sales Manager at
800/777-1048.

Visit our website on the Internet: **www.crossingpress.com**

Library of Congress Cataloging-in-Publication Data

Colbert, Carol.
    Easy French cooking / by Carol Colbert.
        p. cm.
    Includes index.
    ISBN 1-58091-062-9 (pbk.)
    1. Cookery, French. I. Title.

TX719 . C523   2000
641.5944--dc21   99-054230

This book is dedicated to my beloved husband Serge for his endless support. Special thanks to my dear friends and family members who contributed to the creation of this cookbook: Ann, Anne-Sophie, Clayton, Isabelle, Jean, Kimmer, Ljubica, Manu, Michelle, Natacha, Norman, Veronique.

Contents

In every family there are secrets. In my family it's cooking. From my grandmother to my mother, these have been transmitted to my hands. I would like to share these secrets with you, secrets of how to make easy, delicious food. I want to share my family's happiness with you and your family. Some of these recipes have been simplified from the original versions, and I have made some substitutions in ingredients to give you better results, better understanding, and easier preparation. Just try one recipe and you'll understand why this book is entitled, Easy French Cooking.

Bon Appétit!

Carol Colbert

Salads and **Soups**

Cut-Up Raw Vegetables with Garlic Dip
CRUDITÉS AVEC AIOLI

MAKES
ABOUT 1 CUP

Whole mushrooms, diagonal cuts of carrots and celery, disks of yellow turnip (rutabaga), whole radishes, slices of fennel—anything in the vegetable family that you particularly like—can be arranged carefully on a pretty tray with the bowl containing this dip in the center. The dip is also good with any steamed fish.

> 4 garlic cloves
> 1 egg yolk
> 1 tablespoon extra strong Dijon mustard
> ½ teaspoon salt
> Pinch pepper
> 1 cup vegetable oil

1 In a mortar with a pestle, crush the garlic cloves. In a small bowl stir the garlic with the egg yolk and mustard, then add the salt and pepper.

2 Using an electric blender on a very low speed gradually add the oil to the bowl, drop by drop at first, then in a thin stream once it begins to thicken. The dip is ready when it is thick enough to coat the blade of your blender. Store it in a cool place if not used immediately.

Salad Niçoise
SALADE NIÇOISE

This Mediterranean dish is a favorite in my family, particularly for lunch in summertime. The anchovies lend a salty tang to the salad. However, if you don't like anchovies, omit them.

SERVES
4 TO 6

1 butter lettuce
½ pound green beans
4 medium tomatoes, cut in segments
1 12-ounce can tuna fish, packed in oil, drained
4 hard boiled eggs, peeled and quartered
12 anchovy fillets
24 small black olives with pits
½ cup Olive Oil Dressing (see page 21)

1 Wash the lettuce leaves, then dry them. Cut or tear them as desired.

2 Cook the green beans in salted boiling water for 10 minutes or until tender. Drain the beans and cut them in 2-inch lengths.

3 In a large bowl, place the lettuce leaves, beans, tomatoes, tuna, eggs, anchovies, and olives, in that order.

4 Pour the dressing over all, toss, and serve.

Chicken Liver Salad
SALADE AUX FOIES DE VOLAILLE

SERVES 4

For the holidays, you could add a few slices of fois gras as an additional pleasure.

½ pound mixed salad greens
1 pound chicken livers
2 tablespoons vegetable oil
1 tablespoon butter
4 shallots, chopped
Salt and pepper
tomatoes, cut in segments
½ cup Balsamic Dressing (see page 20)

1 Wash and dry the salad greens.

2 Wash the chicken livers, remove the fat if desired, pat dry, and set aside.

3 Heat the oil and butter in a skillet and sauté the shallots until lightly browned.

4 Add the chicken livers, season them with salt and pepper, and fry for about 5 to 8 minutes over high heat.

5 Arrange the greens in a bowl or on individual plates, set the tomatoes on top, then the warm chicken livers and shallots. Pour the dressing on the salad, toss, and serve.

Warm Goat Cheese Salad
SALADE AU CHÊVRE CHAUD

This may be a new idea to many cooks outside of France. It could be a light stand-alone dish for lunch or for a late night meal.

SERVES 4

½ pound mixed salad greens
½ baguette, cut in ½-inch slices
4 ounces soft goat cheese
1 teaspoon dried thyme
1 teaspoon olive oil
½ cup Balsamic Dressing (see page 20)

1 Preheat the oven to broil.

2 Wash the salad greens, then dry them.

3 Broil the baguette slices on a baking sheet for a few minutes. Don't turn off the oven.

4 Spread the goat cheese plentifully on each slice, then sprinkle the thyme and a few drops of olive oil on top. Set aside.

5 Arrange the greens on 4 individual plates, then pour the dressing on top.

6 Warm the goat cheese croutons in the oven, and set on top of salad before serving.

Vegetable Salad
MACÉDOINE DE LÉGUMES

SERVES 4

This is simplicity itself—cubes of root vegetables and string beans boiled, drained and chilled, with homemade mayonnaise as the carrier. This dish works as an appetizer or side dish.

> 4 carrots, in ¼-inch cubes
> 1 turnip, in ¼-inch cubes
> 2 potatoes, in ¼-inch cubes
> ½ pound green beans, in ½-inch lengths
> 1 package frozen peas
> ½ cup mayonnaise (see page 116)
> Salt and pepper

1 Cook all the vegetables in salted boiling water from 10 to 15 minutes or until just tender. Drain and refrigerate them.

2 In a mixing bowl, combine the cold vegetables with the mayonnaise, then correct seasoning if needed.

3 Serve family style in a bowl or on individual plates.

Belgian Endive Salad
SALADE D'ENDIVES AUX NOIX

The combination is what matters here: slivers of delicate endive with walnuts, hard-boiled eggs, and fresh parsley in a mustard dressing. Simple, yet very subtle in texture and taste. A refreshing dish.

SERVES 4

> 5 Belgian endive
> 1 cup walnut halves
> 2 hard-boiled eggs, quartered
> ½ cup Mustard Dressing (see page 19)
> 1 tablespoon chopped fresh parsley

1 Discard the discolored bottoms of the endive, peel off the outer leaves, and wash them under cold water. Pat dry. Slice each endive vertically into 1/2-inch slivers.

2 In a large bowl toss the endive, walnuts, and eggs with the dressing.

3 Sprinkle with parsley and serve.

Seafood Salad
SALADE AUX FRUITS DE MER

SERVES 4

*Homage is paid here to asparagus, the queen of spring veg-
etables. That, plus scallops, mussels, and shrimp with a
lemon dressing — a treat!*

¼ pound mixed salad greens

½ pound thin green asparagus spears

¼ pound mussels

2 tablespoons butter

2 tablespoons olive oil

½ pound scallops

½ pound peeled shrimp

Salt and pepper

4 tablespoons chopped fresh parsley

1 carrot, grated

2 tablespoons salmon roe

½ cup Lemon Dressing (see page 22)

1   Wash the greens, then dry them.

2   Cook the asparagus in salted boiling water for about 10 minutes or until tender, drain, and cut each spear into 2-inch pieces. Set aside.

3   Pull off the beards from the mussels with a quick tug, and wash the mussels under cold water.

4   Place the mussels in a skillet, cover, and cook for about 5 minutes until the shells open up. Remove the meat from the shells. Discard the shells.

5   Heat the butter and oil in a skillet, then sauté the scallops and shrimp for 5 minutes. Season with salt and pepper, sprinkle the seafood with the parsley, and set aside.

6   Arrange the greens on individual plates, place the asparagus, carrot, shrimp, mussels, scallops, and salmon roe. Either pass the dressing separately or pour a thin stream over each plate.

Beef and **Potato Salad**
SALADE À LA PARISIENNE

SERVES 4

This is perfect for a picnic on a spring day, served along with a glass of white wine. Sliced radishes, tomatoes, and cucumber with a simple vinaigrette would be very pleasant on the side. In France we use leftover boiled beef for this dish—in the U.S. corned beef brisket is a very good alternative.

> 2 pounds corned beef brisket, flat cut (with seasoning)
> 5 red potatoes
> ½ red onion, thinly sliced
> ½ cup Mustard Dressing (see page 19)
> 3 hard-boiled eggs, quartered
> 2 tablespoons chopped fresh parsley

1 In a large pot, boil the brisket covered with water and seasoning for about 2 hours or until tender.

2 Meanwhile, in a separate pot boil the potatoes in salted water until cooked. Cool, then peel and cut the potatoes in 1/2-inch-thick slices.

3 Cool the beef, trim the fat, then cut the beef into thin slices.

4 In a mixing bowl, combine the beef, onion and dressing.

5 Transfer the salad to a serving bowl then add the potatoes and eggs and stir gently.

6 Sprinkle with parsley and serve.

The choice of which dressing to use with which ingredients is truly personal. Try each, combine the virtues of one with the virtues of another, and eliminate what you don't like—in other words, experiment to find what suits you.

Mustard Dressing

This is basically a vinaigrette with mustard added for flavor. I'd use it on coleslaw (red and green cabbage) and a salad made primarily of romaine lettuce. The mustard flavor needs to be wedded to something strong enough to take it, like the corned beef in the beef and potato salad.

MAKES
½ CUP

2 tablespoons red wine vinegar

5 tablespoons canola oil

1 tablespoon extra strong Dijon mustard

Salt and pepper

In a small mixing bowl, mix all the ingredients until well combined.

Balsamic Dressing

MAKES
½ CUP

Again, this is a vinaigrette with Balsamic instead of wine vinegar. Balsamic is stronger, more fully bodied than ordinary vinegar, with hints of sweetness as well as sourness. Note that there is less of it in this recipe than the wine vinegar in the preceding recipe. This dressing can be used on any green salad.

> 3 tablespoons balsamic vinegar
> 5 tablespoons canola oil
> Salt and pepper

In a small mixing bowl, mix all the ingredients until well combined.

Olive Oil Dressing

The olive oil is stronger in flavor than the canola oil used in the preceding two recipes. I like this recipe best for all my green salads.

MAKES
½ CUP

2 tablespoons red wine vinegar

5 tablespoons olive oil

1 tablespoon extra strong Dijon mustard

Salt and pepper

In a small mixing bowl, mix all the ingredients until well combined.

Lemon Dressing

MAKES
½ CUP

Here we have a mixture of olive oil and canola oil. The strength of the olive oil is tempered with the canola oil. The lemon juice is fresher in taste than any vinegar.

> Juice of 1 lemon
> 3 tablespoons olive oil
> 2 tablespoons canola oil
> Salt and pepper

In a small mixing bowl, mix all the ingredients until well combined.

Garlic Dressing

The flavor of garlic will predominate here. If you like garlic, it will be your choice. Sometimes I add one or two more cloves to the dressing.

MAKES
½ CUP

1 garlic clove, crushed
3 tablespoons red wine vinegar
2 tablespoons canola oil
3 tablespoons olive oil
Salt and pepper

In a small mixing bowl, mix all the ingredients until well combined.

Herb Dressing

MAKES
½ CUP

This dressing has fresh chives, parsley, and basil—a good combination.

> 1 tablespoon extra strong Dijon mustard
> 2 tablespoons red wine vinegar
> 5 tablespoons canola oil
> 2 tablespoons chopped fresh chives
> 2 tablespoons chopped fresh parsley
> 2 tablespoons chopped fresh basil
> Salt and pepper

In a small mixing bowl, mix all the ingredients until well combined.

Cream of Asparagus Soup
VELOUTÉ AUX ASPERGES

The sour cream and chives add refinement to the taste of this soup.

SERVES 4

  1 pound asparagus
  2 tablespoons butter
  ½ onion, chopped
  4 potatoes, peeled and diced
  3 cups chicken broth
  ½ teaspoon salt
  Pinch pepper
  2 tablespoons sour cream
  2 tablespoons chopped fresh chives

1 Wash and peel the asparagus, then trim off the bottom ends and cut the spears into 2-inch lengths.

2 Melt the butter in a large skillet and sauté the onion. Add the asparagus, then sauté for 5 minutes.

3 Add the potatoes, chicken broth, salt, and pepper to the skillet and stir. Cover and cook for 20 minutes over medium heat.

4 Pour the soup into a food processor, add the sour cream and purée until smooth.

5 Check the seasoning and transfer the soup to a tureen. Sprinkle chives on the soup for garnish.

Onion Soup
SOUPE À L'OIGNON

SERVES 4

Notice that the chicken bouillon used here is a substitute for the French standard beef broth. It will make the soup less hearty, nonetheless very good. It is a tradition in France and in my family to serve onion soup on New Year's Eve.

4 tablespoons butter
4 onions, thinly sliced
3 tablespoons flour
6 cups water
1 chicken bouillon cube
1 teaspoon dried thyme
Salt and pepper
½ baguette, sliced
1 cup grated Swiss cheese

1   Melt the butter in a large skillet and sauté the onions for
    10 to 15 minutes or until softened and lightly browned.

2   Add the flour, water, chicken boullion, thyme, salt, and
    pepper. Cover the skillet, and simmer over a low heat for
    30 minutes. Stir from time to time.

3   Preheat the oven to broil.

4   Broil the baguette slices for 5 minutes on a baking sheet.
    Don't turn off the oven.

5   Pour the soup into 4 heatproof soup bowls. Float 2 slices
    of bread on top of each bowl of soup and then sprinkle
    the cheese on top of each slice.

6   Place the bowls in the oven and broil for 5 minutes or
    until the cheese is melted and lightly browned.

Vegetable Soup with **Basil**
SOUPE AU PISTOU

SERVES 4

This is a great vegetarian main dish. The herb paste is added to the soup just before serving, freshening the broth and intensifying the flavor.

½ pound green beans, cut in 1-inch lengths

3 carrots, cut in 1-inch pieces

3 tomatoes, diced

4 zucchini, diced

1 onion, chopped

2 teaspoons salt

Pinch pepper

4 cups water

½ bunch of fresh basil (about 30 leaves)

5 garlic cloves

6 tablespoons olive oil

1 cup grated Swiss cheese

6 ounces fettuccini

1 Place the beans, carrots, tomatoes, zucchini, onion, salt, and pepper in a large skillet with 4 cups of water, or a quantity sufficient to cover the vegetables. Cook covered for 20 minutes over medium heat.

2 Meanwhile make the basil pesto. Chop the basil leaves. Crush garlic cloves in a mortar and pestle, add the basil,and crush it into a smooth paste. Slowly mix in the olive oil. Add the cheese and stir. Set aside.

3 Break the fettuccini into 2-inch lengths.

4 Add the fettuccini to the soup, and cook uncovered 10 more minutes or until the pasta is cooked.

5 Add the basil pesto to the soup, mix, and serve.

Chilled Leek Soup
VICHYSSOISE

This is good served hot or cold. Your choice will probably be determined by the season.

4 tablespoons butter
1 large leek, white and light green parts only, in
   1-inch pieces
1 onion, chopped
4 medium white potatoes, peeled and cubed
4 cups water
1 chicken bouillon cube
1 teaspoon salt
¼ teaspoon pepper
2 tablespoons chopped fresh chives

1 Melt the butter in a large skillet over medium heat, then sauté the leek, onion, and potatoes for 5 minutes.

2 Decrease the heat, add the water, chicken bouillon cube, salt, and pepper. Cover the skillet and simmer for 30 minutes.

3 In a food processor, blend the soup until creamy and smooth, without lumps.

4 Pour the soup in a tureen; chill at least 30 minutes.

5 Sprinkle chives on top before serving.

Egg Dishes

Ham and Cheese Quiche
QUICHE LORRAINE

SERVES 4

Originally, this quiche required a pastry crust. I have simplified the recipe by adding the flour to the egg and milk mixture. It's quicker to execute and quite good. Ham and Cheese Quiche is one of the most popular dishes in France.

4 slices cooked ham, cut in ½-inch squares

6 bacon strips, cut in ½-inch lengths

½ pound mushrooms, sliced

½ cup flour

1 cup milk

1 cup half-and-half

4 eggs

1 cup grated Swiss cheese

Pinch ground nutmeg

½ teaspoon salt

¼ teaspoon pepper

1 Preheat the oven to 450 °F.

2 Combine the ham and bacon in a skillet and sauté for about 5 minutes. Add the mushrooms to the pan, and sauté 5 more minutes.

3 In a large bowl, mix the flour, milk, half-and-half, eggs, cheese, nutmeg, salt, and pepper.

4 Add the ham, bacon, and mushrooms to the bowl, and stir.

5 Pour the mixture into a 9-inch tart pan and bake for 45 minutes.

6 Serve hot or cold.

Leek Tart
FLAMICHE

SERVES 4

In France we use crème fraîche in this recipe, but since it is not always available in the U.S., I use half-and-half instead. Again, no crust is used. Instead, the flour is added to the eggs to thicken the tart.

> 4 leeks
> ½ cup flour
> 1 cup half-and-half
> 2 eggs, beaten
> 2 tablespoons butter, cut into small pieces
> 1 cup grated Swiss cheese
> ½ teaspoon salt
> Pinch pepper

1 Preheat the oven to 450 °F.

2 Slice the leeks in 1-inch-lengths and wash under cold water. Discard the tough, dark green tops

3 Boil the leeks in salted water for about 10 minutes or until tender; drain.

4 In a large mixing bowl, mix the flour with half-and-half until no lumps appear. Add the eggs, butter, cheese, leeks, salt, and pepper. Mix.

5 Pour the mixture into a greased 9-inch tart pan, and bake for 35 minutes.

6 Serve hot or cold.

Spinach and Eggs au Gratin
GRATIN D'EPINARDS

A very simple recipe, perfect for a Sunday brunch served with a good bread and perhaps herbed butter. The children in my family love this dish.

SERVES 4

2 pounds chopped frozen spinach
1 cup half-and-half
1 chicken bouillon cube
½ teaspoon salt
Large pinch pepper
Pinch ground nutmeg
4 hard-boiled eggs, peeled and cut in half lengthwise
Butter to grease the baking dish

1 Preheat the oven to 400 °F.

2 In a skillet, place the frozen spinach, half-and-half, chicken bouillon cube, salt, pepper, and nutmeg. Cook without a cover over high heat for about 10 minutes. Make sure to stir often to defrost the spinach.

3 Butter an 8 × 8-inch baking dish and spread half of the spinach mixture on the bottom.

4 Arrange the egg halves, rounded side up, on top of the spinach mixture, and spoon the remaining spinach mixture over the eggs.

5 Bake for 30 minutes.

Country Style Omelet
OMELETTE À LA PAYSANNE

SERVES 4

This is akin to a frittata, but there's a difference: the boiled leeks fried with cubed potatoes and bacon are inside the omelet, not mixed together with the eggs and sour cream.

4 medium potatoes, peeled and cut into small cubes

2 leeks

4 tablespoons butter

6 bacon strips, cut in small pieces

6 eggs

2 tablespoons chopped fresh parsley

½ cup grated Swiss cheese

4 tablespoons sour cream

Salt and pepper

1   Cook the potatoes in salted boiled water; drain.

2   Slice the leeks into 1/2-inch pieces, and wash under cold water. Discard the coarse dark green tops.

3   Melt half the butter in a deep frying pan and add the leeks. Cover and cook 10 minutes over a low heat.

4   Add the bacon and sauté for 5 minutes, then add the potatoes and sauté 5 more minutes. Set aside.

5   Beat the eggs in a large mixing bowl, stir in the parsley, cheese, sour cream, salt, and pepper.

6   Heat the remaining butter in an omelet pan over a medium heat, pour in the egg mixture, and cook for about 1 minute. Keep lifting the perimeter of the omelet and twisting the pan so that the uncooked portion will meet the hot skillet. When the omelet is no longer liquid, place the potato-bacon mixture in the center, and fold the omelet over. Cook 1 more minute, and slide onto a serving plate.

Cheese Soufflé
SOUFFLÉ AU FROMAGE

SERVES 4

A soufflé is easy to execute. However there are two difficulties: one, the oven must not be opened for the first 20 minutes or the quiche will not rise; two, it should be served immediately. Don't wait! The soufflé will surely fall.

> 5 tablespoons butter, divided
> 5 eggs
> 4 tablespoons flour
> 1 cup milk
> Large pinch ground nutmeg
> 2 cups grated Swiss cheese
> 1 teaspoon salt
> Large pinch pepper

1 Preheat the oven to 400 °F.

2 Grease a 1-1/2 quarts soufflé dish with 1 tablespoon of butter.

3 Separate the egg yolks from the whites.

4 In a heavy saucepan, melt the remaining butter over medium heat, then whisk in the flour one tablespoon at a time.

5 Decrease the heat and gradually whisk in the milk until the mixture is thick. Take the saucepan off the heat.

6 Stir in the egg yolk and add the nutmeg, cheese, salt, and pepper. Stir vigorously.

7 Beat the egg whites until stiff peaks form.

8 Gently fold the beaten egg whites into the egg yolk-cheese mixture. If you are too vigorous at this point, the soufflé will lose volume.

9 Pour into the greased soufflé dish and bake for 50 minutes. Do not open the oven door the first 20 minutes or the soufflé will not rise. When the soufflé is ready, a knife inserted should come out clean.

10 Serve immediately!

Chicken and Vegetable Terrine
TERRINE DE POULET AUX LÉGUMES

SERVES 6

This terrine is colorful in presentation, with three layers: the white bottom layer of chicken, the orange layer of carrots next, and the top layer of spinach. This is baked, then cut in slices, and served with a simple tomato sauce.

> 7 carrots, peeled and cut in small pieces
> 1 bunch of fresh spinach
> 1 tablespoon vegetable oil
> 3 chicken breasts
> Salt and pepper
> 3 tablespoons sour cream, divided
> 3 eggs, divided
> Butter to grease terrine pan
> 2 cups Tomato Sauce (see page 108)

1 Preheat the oven to 375 °F.

2 Cook the carrots in salted boiling water about 10 minutes or until tender. Drain and set aside.

3 Remove the stems of the spinach, then wash and dry. Put the spinach in salted boiling water and cook until tender.

4 Heat the oil in a skillet and fry the chicken about 3 minutes on each side. Season with salt and pepper, and cut in small pieces. Set aside.

5   In a food processor, place the carrots, 1 tablespoon sour cream, and 1 egg. Blend until creamy. Set aside.

6   Clean the food processor and repeat the procedure with the spinach.

7   Clean the food processor and repeat the procedure with the chicken.

8   Grease a 12 × 5-inch terrine pan with butter.

9   First lay chicken mixture on the bottom of the dish, then lay the carrot mixture, and finish with the spinach.

10 Set the terrine in a double-boiler or "bain-marie" and bake for 1 hour.

11 While the terrine is baking, make the Tomato Sauce (see page 108).

12 Unmold the terrine on a large plate. The spinach should be on top. It will be easier to slice that way.

13 Wait until the terrine cools down. Then cut it in 1/2-inch pieces.

14 Presentation: Set 2 slices of the terrine in the center of each plate and spoon hot Tomato Sauce around them.

Chicken, Beef, Veal, and Lamb Entrées

Chicken Stuffed with Tarragon
Poulet Farci à l'Estragon

SERVES 4

I like to roast a chicken, perhaps a capon, and stuff it with tarragon and garlic. It can be done relatively quickly, depending on the weight of the chicken.

2 tablespoons butter

1 chicken (3-4 pounds)

4 tablespoons chopped fresh tarragon

1 garlic clove, minced

1 teaspoon salt, divided

¼ teaspoon pepper

1 teaspoon olive oil

1 teaspoon dried thyme

1 Preheat the oven to 400 °F.

2 Cut the butter in small pieces.

3 Rinse the chicken under cold water, then pat dry.

4 In a small mixing bowl, combine the pieces of butter, tarragon, garlic, 1/2 teaspoon salt, and pepper. Stuff this mixture into the chicken's body cavity.

5 Place the chicken, breast side up, in a roasting pan and brush it with olive oil. Sprinkle the rest of the salt and the thyme over the bird and roast it until done. Pierce the chicken thigh with a fork. The juices should run clear.

6 Baste chicken with pan juice from time to time. Use the juice in the roasting pan as a sauce, served in a small pitcher at the table.

Chicken in Red Wine
Coq au Vin

SERVES 4

A whole chicken, cut up, is browned in bacon fat and then simmered in red wine with shallots, onions, and mushrooms. In France, this is called Coq au Vin—"coq" is French for rooster. These days it is easier to get a big fryer.

6 bacon strips, diced

¾ pound small onions, peeled

4 shallots, chopped

1 fryer chicken (3-4 pounds), cut into 8 pieces

2 tablespoons flour

3 cups red wine (Bordeaux, Cabernet)

1 cup water

2 unpeeled whole garlic cloves

1 teaspoon dried thyme

1 bay leaf

Pinch ground nutmeg

½ pound mushrooms, sliced

1 teaspoon salt

¼ teaspoon pepper

1   In a large, heavy skillet sauté the bacon, onions, and shallots for about 3 minutes.

2   Sauté the chicken for 5 more minutes until it turns light brown.

3   Decrease the heat and add the flour, wine, water, garlic, thyme, bay leaf, nutmeg, mushrooms, salt, and pepper. Cover and simmer for 40 minutes.

4   Remove the cover and simmer 30 more minutes.

5   Discard the bay leaf before serving and correct the seasoning.

Chicken with **Red** and **Green Peppers**
POULET BASQUAISE

SERVES 4

A whole chicken, cut up, is browned in oil, then simmered with pepper strips, onions, garlic, and tomatoes. This dish takes under an hour to prepare. You can make this several hours ahead and then reheat it just before dinner. Basmati rice would be a good accompaniment.

> 1 green pepper
> 1 red pepper
> 2 large tomatoes
> 2 tablespoons olive oil
> 1 fryer chicken (3-4 pounds), cut into 8 pieces
> 1 onion, chopped
> 2 chopped garlic cloves
> 1 tablespoon tomato paste
> 1 teaspoon salt
> ¼ teaspoon pepper

1 Cut the peppers in half, lengthwise, and scrape out the seeds and cores. Discard these.

2 Slice each pepper lengthwise into 1/2-inch-thick strips.

3 Cut the tomatoes into small pieces.

4 Heat the oil in a heavy, large pan, then sauté the chicken pieces until brown.

5 Reduce the heat, add the pepper strips, tomatoes, onion, garlic, tomato paste, salt, and pepper.

6 Cover and cook for about 40 minutes over low heat, stirring from time to time.

Chicken with Mushrooms and Tomatoes
POULET SAUTÉ À LA CHASSEUR

SERVES 4

This simple stew of chicken simmered in dry white wine and tomatoes can be prepared in little more than one hour.

2 tablespoons olive oil

1 onion, chopped

4 chicken thighs

½ cup dry white wine

1 pound mushrooms, sliced

1 cup chicken broth, canned or fresh

1 tablespoon tomato paste

½ teaspoon dried thyme

4 tomatoes, cubed

1 bay leaf

½ tablespoon flour

¾ teaspoon salt

¼ teaspoon pepper

4 tablespoons chopped fresh parsley

1 Heat the oil in a large, heavy skillet and sauté the onion until golden brown.

2 Add the chicken and sauté about 5 minutes over high heat.

3 Decrease the heat to low, add the wine, and simmer the chicken so that the alcohol in the wine will evaporate, about 5 minutes.

4 In the same skillet, add the mushrooms, chicken broth, tomato paste, thyme, tomatoes, bay leaf, flour, salt, and pepper. Cover and cook over a medium heat for 15 minutes.

5 Sprinkle the parsley on the chicken and cook, uncovered, 45 more minutes over low heat.

6 Correct the seasoning if needed and discard the bay leaf before serving.

Chicken Braised in White Wine
FRICASSÉ DE POULET AU VIN BLANC

The chicken is sautéed, then simmered in wine. The cream cheese added to the resulting sauce adds creaminess and richness. Steamed small red potatoes with the skins on would be good with this dish.

2 tablespoons butter
2 shallots, chopped
1 onion, chopped
4 pounds boneless, skinless chicken breasts
1 cup dry white wine
½ pound mushrooms, sliced
½ cup water
1 bay leaf
1 teaspoon dried thyme
Salt and pepper
2 tablespoons cream cheese

1 In a large, deep skillet, melt the butter, then sauté the shallots and onion. Add the chicken breasts and sauté each side for about 5 minutes.

2 Decrease the heat to low. Add the wine and let the alcohol evaporate for 5 minutes.

3 Add the mushrooms, water, bay leaf, thyme, salt, and pepper. Cover and cook for about 30 minutes.

4 Stir in the cream cheese.

5 Simmer uncovered 10 more minutes.

6 Discard the bay leaf and adjust the seasoning before serving.

Chicken in a Creamy Blue Cheese Sauce
SUPRÊMES DE VOLAILLE AU ROQUEFORT

SERVES 4

This recipe is similar to the preceding one, but here the blue cheese is mixed into the cream cheese sauce.

2 tablespoons butter
4 chicken breasts, boneless, skinless
2 shallots, chopped
1 cup dry white wine
½ cup water
8 tablespoons cream cheese (4 oz.)
Salt and pepper
6 tablespoons crumbled blue cheese (2 oz.)

1 Melt the butter in a deep frying pan and sauté the chicken breasts 3 minutes on each side over high heat. Set the chicken aside.

2 In the same pan, sauté the shallots until light brown. Decrease heat to low. Add the wine and water. Simmer this without a cover for about 5 minutes until the liquid in the pan is reduced.

3 Stir in the cream cheese. Add the chicken and season it with salt and pepper, cover, and simmer 20 minutes more over low heat.

4 In a small mixing bowl, combine the blue cheese with 4 tablespoons of the sauce in the pan. Crush the blue cheese so that the paste is creamy and smooth. Pour this mixture into the pan and mix the chicken and sauce gently.

Filets Mignon with Béarnaise Sauce

FILETS MIGNONS AVEC SAUCE BÉARNAISE

SERVES 4

The sauce is complex here: white wine, red wine vinegar, shallots, and fresh tarragon.

2 tablespoons butter
2 cups Béarnaise Sauce (see page 112)
4 filets mignon
Salt and pepper

1 Melt the butter in a large skillet and fry the steaks.

Rare: 2 minutes on each side.
Medium rare: 4 minutes on each side.
Medium: 5 minutes on each side.
Well done: 6 minutes on each side.

2 While the steaks are cooking, warm up the Béarnaise Sauce.

3 Season steaks with salt and pepper. Arrange the steaks on individual plates and either pass the sauce on the side or pour some around each steak.

Filets Mignon with Shallots and Red Wine Sauce
FILETS MIGNONS AVEC SAUCE BORDELAISE

The red wine sauce makes this dish.

SERVES 4

2 tablespoons butter (¼ stick)
4 filets mignon
Salt and pepper
2 cups Shallots and Red Wine Sauce (see page 111)

1 Melt the butter in a large frying pan. Season the steaks with salt and pepper.

2 Fry the steaks according to taste.

Rare: 2 minutes on each side.
Medium rare: 4 minutes on each side.
Medium: 5 minutes on each side.
Well done: 6 minutes on each side.

3 While the steaks are cooking, warm up the shallots and Red Wine Sauce.

4 Arrange the steaks on individual plates with sauce on the side or in a gravy boat.

Tenderloin of Beef in Pastry

FILET DE BOEUF EN CROÛTE

SERVES 4

An elegant dish, perfect for company, an improvement on Beef Wellington.

> 1 frozen puff pastry sheet (8 oz.)
> 4 tablespoons butter
> 2 pounds beef tenderloin, in one piece
> Salt and pepper
> 1 beaten egg

1 Defrost the puff pastry and preheat the oven to 475 °F.

2 Melt the butter in a deep frying pan and sauté the meat for about 2 minutes on each side. Season it with salt and pepper.

3 Place the meat in a baking dish and carefully cover it with the puff pastry. Brush the pastry with the beaten egg.

4 Using a knife, pierce the pastry to prevent it from cracking, then bake 40 minutes for medium-rare meat or 50 minutes for well-done meat.

5 Cool the tenderloin for a few minutes before carving it. Cut it with an electric knife or a very sharp carving knife. Thick slices are best.

NOTE : recommend Béarnaise Sauce or Shallots and Red Wine Sauce with this dish.

Beef Burgundy
BOEUF BOURGUIGNON

This basically simple stew takes over two hours to make. Bacon fat is used for the frying and Bordeaux for the liquid.

SERVES 4

2 celery stalks in ½-inch lengths
8 bacon strips in ½-inch lengths
¾ pound pearl onions
2 pounds boneless stewing beef, cut in 2-inch pieces
½ pound baby carrots
1 tablespoon flour
2 teaspoons salt
½ teaspoon pepper
1 teaspoon dried thyme
1 bay leaf
4 garlic cloves
2 cups red wine (Bordeaux)
1 tablespoon tomato paste

1 In a large skillet, sauté the celery, bacon, and onions over medium heat.

2 Increase the heat to high, add the beef, and sauté for 5 minutes.

3 Decrease the heat to very low, stir in the carrots and flour. Then add the salt, pepper, thyme, bay leaf, garlic cloves, wine, and tomato paste. Cover and simmer for 2 hours.

4 Discard the bay leaf before serving.

Steak with Green Peppercorn Sauce

STEAK AU POIVRE VERT

SERVES 4

This will be a surprise for the people who go to steak houses. Cognac and heavy cream provide the sauce, green peppercorns the spice.

4 tablespoons green peppercorns (drained from a jar or can)

4 New York steaks

2 tablespoons butter

2 tablespoons vegetable oil

2 tablespoons cognac

1 cup heavy whipping cream

Salt

1 Crush the peppercorns in a mortar and pestle. Rub the steaks with the resulting paste on both sides.

2 In a frying pan, melt the butter with the oil and cook the steaks according to your taste:

Rare: 2 minutes on each side.
Medium rare: 4 minutes on each side.
Medium: 5 minutes on each side.
Well done: 6 minutes on each side

3 Remove the steaks from the pan and keep them warm. Discard the grease in the pan.

4 In the same pan heat the cognac for about 2 minutes, and keep stirring until the sauce begins to thicken.

5 Add the cream and mix gently.

6 Set the steaks on plates, season them with salt and pepper, and coat them with sauce.

Boiled Beef with Vegetables
POT-AU-FEU

SERVES 4-6

This is a meal in itself, with the broth served before the beef and vegetables. Note there is only one pot to wash — there is no sautéing necessary. It does take two hours, but you can busy yourself with other matters while it is on the stove. A very popular, simple French dish.

2 pounds boneless chuck, cut into 2-inch pieces

2 onions

2 cloves

8 purple turnips, peeled and cut in half

1 celery stalk, cut in ½-inch lengths

1 leek, white and light green parts only

½ pound baby carrots

2 garlic cloves, skin on

1 tablespoon salt

½ teaspoon pepper

6 white potatoes, peeled and halved

1 Place the meat in a heavy skillet with sufficient water enough to cover it. When it starts to boil, skim the scum off the surface.

2 Take each onion and insert a clove.

3 Add the onions, turnips, celery, leek, carrots, garlic, salt, and pepper to the skillet. Cover and cook over medium heat for an hour and a half.

4 Add the potatoes to the skillet and cook 30 minutes longer.

5 Start the meal with the broth. Serve the meat and vegetables as a second course.

Beef Stew Provençal
DAUBE À LA PROVENÇALE

SERVES 4

Like the recipe for Beef Burgundy, bacon is used for the frying. However, the recipes differ in that wine vinegar is added, along with a small strip of orange rind for fragrance and a touch of bitterness.

 5 bacon strips, diced
 2 pounds boneless stewing beef, cut in 2-inch cubes
 2 garlic cloves
 1 teaspoon flour
 2 carrots, cut in ½-inch lengths
 2 onions, chopped
 1 bay leaf
 2 cups red wine
 5 tablespoons red wine vinegar
 1 teaspoon dried thyme
 1 teaspoon tomato paste
 1 cup of water
 1 small strip orange rind
 1 teaspoon salt
 ½ teaspoon pepper

1   Sauté the bacon in a heavy skillet over medium heat until brown. Add the beef and garlic, and sauté 5 more minutes.

2   Add the flour, carrots, onions, bay leaf, wine, vinegar, thyme, tomato paste, water, orange rind, salt, and pepper. Simmer covered over very low heat for 3 hours.

3   Stir from time to time and check the seasoning before serving.

Ground Beef Casserole
HACHI-PARMENTIER

SERVES 4

*This is like the British shepherd's pie with a difference —
the French put grated Swiss cheese with the ground beef
and on top of the casserole*

8 peeled potatoes
2 tablespoons butter, divided
1 onion, chopped
2 shallots, chopped
1 ½ pounds ground beef
2 tablespoons tomato paste
¼ cup water
4 tablespoons chopped fresh parsley
1 teaspoon salt
¼ teaspoon pepper
1 cup milk
Pinch nutmeg
2 cups grated Swiss cheese, divided

1   Preheat the oven to 450 °F.

2   Cut the potatoes in quarters and cook in salted water until soft. Drain and set aside.

3   Melt half the butter in a frying pan and sauté the onion and shallots until lightly brown.

4   Add the meat and sauté 5 more minutes.

5   Decrease the heat, add the tomato paste, 1/4 cup water, parsley, salt, and pepper. Cover and simmer for 10 minutes.

6   Place the potatoes in a mixing bowl and crush with a fork or potato masher. Stir in the milk, the remaining butter, nutmeg, and half the Swiss cheese. Adjust the seasoning if needed.

7   Grease an 8 × 8-inch baking dish with butter and lay the ground beef mixture on the bottom. Place the mashed potatoes on the top. Level the potato layer.

8   Sprinkle the remaining cheese on top and bake for 30 minutes.

Beef Braised with Carrots
BOEUF AUX CAROTTES

SERVES 4

The beef is sautéed first in oil. Note the seasonings: sugar, thyme, and bay leaf.

2 tablespoons vegetable oil

2 pounds boneless stewing beef, cut in 2-inch cubes

2 tablespoons butter

2 pounds peeled baby carrots

1 onion, chopped

2 garlic cloves, peels on

1 teaspoon sugar

1 teaspoon salt

¼ teaspoon pepper

2 cups warm water

1 bay leaf

½ teaspoon dried thyme

1 Heat the oil in a heavy skillet and sauté the meat about 5 minutes, until it is brown. Set it aside.

2 In the same skillet, melt the butter over medium heat, add the carrots, onion, garlic cloves, sugar, salt and pepper, and sauté for 5 minutes.

3 Return the meat to the skillet, and add the water, bay leaf, and thyme. Cover the pan and simmer for 1 hour over low heat.

4 Discard the bay leaf and adjust the seasoning before serving.

Roasted Leg of Lamb with **Potatoes**
GIGOT D'AGNEAU AUX POMMES DE TERRE

This is a very simple recipe, really foolproof. Your success will depend on the quality of the lamb you purchase. The only recourse is to get a good butcher and trust him.

SERVES 6

1 leg of lamb (about 5 pounds)
6 garlic cloves
3 pounds small potatoes, cut in quarters
6 tablespoons vegetable oil
1 teaspoon salt
¼ teaspoon pepper
1 teaspoon dried thyme
2 teaspoons chopped fresh rosemary
½ cup water

1 Preheat the oven to 450 °F.

2 Rinse the leg of lamb under cold water, then pat dry.

3 Using a knife, cut 6 small slits all over the lamb. Place a clove of garlic in each slit.

4 Grease a roasting pan, and put the lamb in it. Place the potatoes around the lamb, pour the oil over all, and season with salt, pepper, thyme, and rosemary. Add the water and roast for 1 hour or longer if you wish the lamb to be well done.

5 Rest the lamb at room temperature for 15 minutes.

Braised Lamb with Vegetables

NAVARIN D'AGNEAU

SERVES
4 TO 6

This is an interesting lamb stew with tomatoes, turnips, potatoes, peas, and carrots.

4 tablespoons vegetable oil

2 pounds lamb sirloin chops, boned and cut into
  2-inch pieces

2 tablespoons flour

2 cups water

2 fresh tomatoes, cut into quarters

1 teaspoon dried thyme

1 bay leaf

2 garlic cloves

1 tablespoon tomato paste

1 onion, chopped

2 teaspoons salt

1 teaspoon pepper

¼ pound small turnips, peeled and cut in quarters

1 pound small potatoes, peeled

1 package frozen peas, defrosted

½ pound baby carrots

1 In a heavy skillet heat the oil and sauté the lamb until it is brown.

2 Stir in the flour and fry for about 2 minutes.

3 Add the water, tomatoes, thyme, bay leaf, garlic cloves, tomato paste, onion, salt, and pepper. Bring to a boil, then decrease the heat. Cover and simmer for 1 hour over low heat.

4 Add all the vegetables to the skillet, increase the heat to medium, and cook uncovered for 40 minutes, stirring from time to time.

Veal Stew
BLANQUETTE DE VEAU

SERVES 4

Here the meat is boiled first, then sautéed in butter, then re-turned to the pot with the vegetables and simmered. Egg yolks are added to thicken the sauce at the last. Rice is particularly good with this stew.

2 pounds boneless veal, in 2-inch cubes

1 cup dry white wine

2 cups water

1 whole onion

2 cloves

½ pound baby carrots, peeled

2 garlic cloves with skins on

½ teaspoon dried thyme

1 bay leaf

1 teaspoon salt

¼ teaspoon pepper

4 tablespoons butter

3 tablespoons flour

2 egg yolks

Juice of half a lemon

4 tablespoons chopped fresh parsley

1 Place the veal in a skillet with the wine and 2 cups of water. When it starts to boil, skim the scum off the surface.

2 Meanwhile, stud the onion with the cloves.

3 Reduce the heat under the skillet, add the onion, carrots, garlic, thyme, bay leaf, salt, and pepper. Cover and simmer over low heat for 45 minutes.

4 Turn off the heat. Remove the meat from the broth and set aside.

5 In a separate skillet, melt the butter over medium heat, add the veal, and brown it on all sides.

6 Add the flour and stir gently.

7 Add the broth with the vegetables to the skillet, cover, and cook over a low heat for 45 minutes.

8 In a small mixing bowl, combine the egg yolks with the lemon juice, and 2 tablespoons of the broth. Pour this mixture into the skillet. Add the parsley and stir.

9 Discard the onion and bay leaf before serving.

Veal Scaloppine with Morel Mushrooms

ESCALOPES DE VEAU AUX MORILLES

SERVES 4

The veal scallops are fried quickly in butter, then sautéed with dried morel mushrooms or porcini mushrooms (cêpes) and heavy cream. The cream is a substitute for crème fraîche.

1 ounce dried morel mushrooms

1 ½ cups warm water, divided

4 tablespoons butter, divided

½ chicken bouillon cube

Salt and pepper

2 tablespoons heavy whipping cream

4 veal scallops

1 In a bowl, combine the mushrooms with 1 cup of the warm water and let stand about 20 minutes until the mushrooms become soft.

2 Drain the mushrooms and pat dry.

3 Melt half the butter in a deep frying pan. Sauté the mushrooms for 2 minutes, add the remaining 1/2 cup of water, and the bouillon cube. Season with salt and pepper, and simmer uncovered for 10 minutes over very low heat.

4 Add the whipping cream and cook a few minutes.

5 Melt the remaining butter in a separate frying pan and cook the scallops for about 3 minutes on each side, depending on their thickness.

6 Add the mushrooms with their sauce to the meat and stir for 2 minutes.

7 Arrange the scallops and the mushrooms on individual plates and coat with the sauce.

Braised Veal in White Wine Sauce
SAUTÉ DE VEAU À LA CHASSEUR

The veal is sautéed first, then stewed in white wine.

4 tablespoons butter, divided
2 pounds boneless veal, cut in 2-inch cubes
1 teaspoon salt
¼ teaspoon pepper
1 onion, chopped
2 tablespoons flour
1 cup dry white wine
1 tablespoon tomato paste
2 teaspoons dried thyme
1 bay leaf
2 cups water
4 shallots, chopped
¼ pound mushrooms, sliced
4 tablespoons chopped fresh parsley

1. Melt half the butter in a big skillet and sauté the veal over high heat.

2. When the veal turns brown, season it with salt and pepper. Add the onion and flour, and stir. Then add the wine, tomato paste, thyme, bay leaf, and water. Cover and simmer over low heat for 1 hour.

3. In a small skillet, melt the remaining butter and sauté the shallots and mushrooms for about 5 minutes.

4. Add the shallots and mushrooms to the skillet containing the veal. Add the parsley and simmer for 10 more minutes.

Fish and Seafood Entrées

Salmon Fillet in Red Wine Sauce
FILET DE SAUMON SAUCE VIN ROUGE

SERVES 4

The salmon fillets are sautéed and then placed on plates coated with an elaborately seasoned red wine sauce.

3 shallots, chopped

2 cups red wine

1 carrot, peeled and sliced thin

1 tomato, diced

Pinch dried thyme

1 garlic clove

1 bay leaf

3 sprigs fresh parsley

Pinch ground nutmeg

1 small strip lemon rind

½ cup water

½ teaspoon salt

Large pinch pepper

1 tablespoon flour

1 teaspoon butter

2 tablespoons olive oil

4 salmon fillets

1   Combine the shallots and wine in a saucepan and bring to a boil.

2   Reduce the heat to very low, add the carrot, tomato, thyme, garlic, bay leaf, parsley, nutmeg, lemon rind, water, salt, and pepper.

3   Whisk in the flour until smooth and without lumps, and cook uncovered for 40 minutes. Put the mixture through a sieve. Discard the flavoring ingredients. Return the sauce to the pan, stir in the butter, and keep it hot.

4   Heat the oil in a skillet and fry the salmon steaks 5 minutes on each side.

5   Place the steaks on individual plates coated with red wine sauce.

Salmon in Aspic
BAVAROIS DE SAUMON

An elegant first course dish, beautiful in presentation.

1 envelope unflavored gelatin

½ cup water

12 ounces smoked salmon slices

2 cups heavy whipping cream, divided

4 teaspoons chopped fresh dill

2 tablespoons salmon eggs

½ teaspoon salt

Pinch pepper

Juice of 2 limes

1 Combine the gelatin with the cold water in a saucepan. Over low heat, stir for about 5 minutes or until the gelatin is dissolved.

2 Cover the inside of four 4-inch round molds with salmon, making sure the slices hang over the lip of the bowl.

3 Set aside any leftover salmon slices and cut them in pieces.

4 Whip 1 cup whipping cream until stiff, then stir in the gelatin, chopped salmon, dill, salmon eggs, salt, and pepper.

5 Fill each mold with the cream preparation and fold the hanging salmon slices inside the bowl.

6 Wrap the bowls with plastic and chill for about 3 hours.

7 When you are ready to serve this dish, combine the remaining whipping cream with the lime juice.

8 On each serving plate unmold the salmon aspic, then delicately pour the cream and lime juice mixture around the aspic.

Salmon Fillet in a Sorrel Sauce
FILET DE SAUMON À L'OSEILLE

SERVES 4

Here the salmon is sautéed briefly and then cooked in the sauce.

4 tablespoons butter

4 salmon fillets

1 bunch fresh sorrel leaves, minced

1 leek, white and light green parts only, cut in ½-inch lengths

1 cup dry white wine

4 tablespoons sour cream

1 teaspoon salt

¼ teaspoon pepper

1   Melt the butter in a large skillet and sauté the fillets for 2 minutes on each side over medium heat, starting with the skin side up.

2   Decrease the heat to low, add the sorrel leaves, leek, wine, sour cream, salt, and pepper. Cook uncovered for 5 minutes, then cook covered for about 10 to 15 more minutes.

Trout with Parsley

TRUITE MEUNIÈRE

This dish is very simple. Just sauté the trout encased in flour. The sauce is merely more butter, lemon juice, and parsley poured into the same frying pan.

SERVES 4

    4 trout

    4 tablespoons flour

    2 tablespoons vegetable oil

    Salt and pepper

    4 tablespoons butter

    Juice of 1 lemon

    8 tablespoons chopped parsley

1 Rinse trout and pat dry. Coat each trout with flour.

2 Heat the oil in a large skillet over medium heat, and fry the trout about 4 to 6 minutes on each side, depending on their thickness.

3 Season the trout with salt and pepper, remove from the pan, and keep warm on serving plates.

4 Melt the butter in the same skillet and, stir in the lemon juice and parsley. Pour the butter sauce over the trout and serve.

Fish Soup
SOUPE DE POISSON

SERVES 4

If you strain the soup, you will have a moderately smooth texture. If you let the pieces of vegetables be more or less intact, you will have a more peasant-like fish stew. Any white meat fish will do, like cod, snapper or sole. At least two kinds of fish should be used for this dish.

4 tablespoons olive oil

1 onion, chopped

1 leek, white and light green parts only, cut in 1-inch lengths

3 garlic cloves, chopped, divided

2 tablespoons tomato paste

4 cups water

1 bay leaf

1 teaspoon ground fennel

Pinch powdered or thread saffron

1 teaspoon salt

¼ teaspoon pepper

2 pounds of white fish fillets
(4 red snapper fillets, 1 lb.)
(4 skinned sole fillets, 1 lb.)

½ Baguette

1 cup grated Swiss cheese

1   In a large skillet, heat the oil, and sauté the onion, leek, and garlic for 2 minutes over high heat until they are softened.

2   Add the tomato paste, water, bay leaf, fennel, saffron, salt, and pepper. Cover and cook over medium heat for 10 minutes.

3   Meanwhile cut the fish in large pieces. Add the fish to the skillet, reduce the heat to very low, cover, and cook for 40 minutes.

4   Heat the oven to broil.

5   Slice the bread. Scrape each slice with the remaining clove of garlic and sprinkle the cheese on the top of each slice. Broil the slices.

6   Purée the soup in a blender, then pass through a sieve.

7   Pour the soup in a tureen and float the bread slices. Serve.

Fish Stew
BOUILLABAISSE

SERVES 6

I advise serving the fish separately from the broth and potatoes. There are three pounds of fish required here for a fish-filled stew. This is a typical entrée from Provence, where it is made with local fish from the Mediterranean. You'll need a bib when you encounter this stew.

3 pounds white fish
    1 halibut fillet, 1 lb.
    2 red snapper fillets, ½ lb.
    2 cod fillets, ½ lb.
    1 sea bass steak, 1 lb.
1 cup Spicy Provençal Sauce (see page 114)
½ baguette, sliced and toasted
1 cup grated Swiss cheese
4 tablespoons olive oil
1 leek, white and light green parts only, cut in ½-inch lengths
2 onions, chopped
4 garlic cloves, chopped
2 fresh tomatoes, chopped
1 teaspoon dried thyme
2 teaspoons dried fennel
2 tablespoons chopped fresh parsley
2 bay leaves
1 small strip orange rind
Large pinch powdered saffron

6 red potatoes, cut in ½-inch slices
1 ½ teaspoons salt
¼ teaspoon pepper
5 cups hot water

1 Rinse the fish and pat dry.

2 Spread the Spicy Provençal Sauce over the bread slices and sprinkle each slice with cheese. Set aside.

3 In a large skillet, heat the oil and sauté the leek and onions until tender. Decrease the heat and add the garlic, tomatoes, thyme, fennel, parsley, bay leaves, orange rind, saffron, and potatoes.

4 Season with salt and pepper, and add the water. Cook covered for 10 minutes.

5 Place the fish into the skillet and simmer for 10–15 minutes.

6 Using a spatula, carefully lift the fish from the skillet and place on a serving dish.

7 Serve the broth and potatoes in a soup tureen with bread slices floating on top. Serve the fish separately.

Stuffed Mussels on the Half Shell

MOULES FARCIES

SERVES 4

This is easy to prepare, and charming in presentation.

2 sticks butter, cut in small pieces
10 tablespoons chopped fresh parsley
6 garlic cloves, chopped
1 teaspoon salt
Large pinch pepper
4 pounds fresh mussels

1 Preheat the oven to 400 °F.

2 In a mixing bowl, combine the butter, parsley, garlic, salt, and pepper.

3 Pull off the beard from each mussel with a quick tug, then wash under cold water.

4 Place the mussels in a large skillet, cover, and cook over medium-high heat for about 5 minutes or until the shells open up.

5 Pull chopped shells apart and discard the shells that do not contain meat.

6 Stuff the mussels by placing 1/2 teaspoon of the butter mixture on top of each mussel.

7 Place the mussels in a shallow baking dish and bake for 5 minutes.

Mussels in White Wine
MOULES MARINIÈRES

This is similar to what the Belgians do with mussels, except they use more herbs. French fried potatoes are wonderful with this.

SERVES 4

4 pounds fresh mussels
1 tablespoon butter
4 shallots, chopped
1 cup dry white wine
6 tablespoons chopped fresh parsley
Pepper

1. Pull the beards off each mussel with a quick tug and wash under cold water.

2. Melt the butter in a large skillet, then sauté the shallots for about 2 minutes over medium heat.

3. Add the mussels to the skillet, pour in the wine, and cook covered over medium heat for 10 minutes.

4. At this point all the shells should be open. Sprinkle the mussels with chopped parsley, season with pepper, and serve.

Seafood Quiche
QUICHE AUX FRUITS DE MER

SERVES 4

1 pound fresh mussels

2 tablespoons butter

½ pound bay scallops

3 eggs

2 cups milk

⅔ cup flour

2 tablespoons sour cream

4 tablespoons chopped fresh parsley

½ teaspoon salt

Large pinch pepper

¼ pound cooked shrimp

1 Preheat the oven to 450 °F.

2 Pull the beards off each mussel with a quick tug and wash under cold water.

3 Place the mussels in a large skillet, cover, and cook over medium-high heat for about 5 minutes, or until the shells open up. Remove the meat from the shells. Discard the shells.

4 Melt 1 tablespoon of butter in a frying pan and sauté the scallops. Set aside.

5 In a large mixing bowl, mix the eggs, milk, flour, sour cream, parsley, salt, and pepper. Whisk until the mixture is smooth, then add the mussels, shrimp, and scallops.

6 Grease a 9-inch quiche pan with the rest of the butter, pour the quiche preparation into a pan and bake 50 minutes or until a toothpick inserted in the center comes out clean.

7 Serve either hot or cold.

Vegetable Dishes

Mashed Potatoes
PURÉE DE POMMES DE TERRE

SERVES 4

This is the All-American standard, but with a French twist. The additions of the whipping cream, nutmeg, and Swiss cheese really gild the lily.

> 2 pounds potatoes, peeled and quartered
> 2 cups milk
> 4 tablespoons whipping cream
> 4 tablespoons butter
> Pinch ground nutmeg
> Salt and pepper
> Grated Swiss cheese (optional)

1 Place the potatoes into a large pan with salted water, enough to cover, and cook for about 15 minutes or until softened.

2 Meanwhile, heat the milk until very hot.

3 Drain the potatoes and place them in a large mixing bowl. Then mash them with a fork or potato masher until they are smooth.

4 Stir in the hot milk and whipping cream.

5 Add the butter, nutmeg, salt, and pepper, and mix until combined.

6 Sprinkle with the cheese if you wish.

Gratinéed Scalloped Potatoes
GRATIN DAUPHINOIS

This is good served as a side dish with filets of fish, or steak. I've substituted half-and-half for crème fraîche, which is not readily available in this country.

SERVES 4

8 red potatoes
2 cups half-and-half
2 cups grated Swiss cheese (½ pound), divided
2 garlic cloves, chopped
Pinch ground nutmeg
1 teaspoon salt
Large pinch pepper
Butter to grease baking dish

1 Preheat the oven to 375 °F.

2 Peel and cut the potatoes into 1/4-inch slices.

3 In a large mixing bowl, combine the potatoes, half-and-half, 1 cup cheese, garlic, nutmeg, salt, and pepper.

4 Grease an 8 × 8-inch baking dish with butter.

5 Fill the baking dish with the potato mixture and sprinkle the remaining cheese on top.

6 Bake for 1 1/2 hours.

Creamed Spinach
EPINARDS À LA CRÈME

SERVES 4

I've noticed that Americans tend to cook their vegetables more quickly than we do. You may want to taste a leaf of spinach after a few minutes to see if it is done to your satisfaction.

2 bunches fresh spinach
2 tablespoons butter
1 tablespoon flour
1 cup half-and-half
½ chicken bouillon cube
Large pinch nutmeg
Salt and pepper

1   Wash the spinach. Discard everything but the leaves.

2   Boil the spinach leaves in a little water with salt added for 10 minutes. Drain and set aside.

3   In a large saucepan, melt the butter, stir in the flour, pour in the half-and-half, and keep stirring until all the lumps are dissolved.

4   Add the chicken bouillon cube, nutmeg, salt, pepper, and spinach, and cook uncovered for about 10 minutes over low heat.

Tomatoes with Garlic and Parsley
TOMATES À LA PROVENÇALE

This is a very simple, very good recipe, wonderful with a steak, fried fish, anything at all—including a grilled cheese sandwich.

SERVES 4

10 ripe tomatoes
4 tablespoons olive oil
Salt and pepper
4 tablespoons chopped fresh parsley
6 garlic cloves, chopped

1 Core the tomatoes and cut them in half vertically. Squeeze them to remove the seeds, using your hand.

2 Heat the oil in a large frying pan and arrange the tomato halves rounded side down. Cook over medium heat for 20 minutes.

3 Turn the tomatoes over, season with salt and pepper, sprinkle with parsley and garlic, cover, and cook 20 more minutes.

Broccoli Purée
MOUSSELINE DE BROCOLIS

SERVES 4

The egg provides the glue that holds this together. Note that it is placed in the oven.

1 ½ pounds broccoli florets
1 egg
Salt and pepper
3 tablespoons whipping cream
Pinch ground nutmeg
1 tablespoon butter

1   Preheat the oven to 400 °F.

2   Boil the broccoli in salted water for about 10 minutes or until tender. Drain.

3   Combine the broccoli with the egg in a food processor.

4   Add the salt, pepper, whipping cream, and nutmeg. Then blend until thoroughly combined.

5   Grease a terrine mold with butter.

6   Pour the broccoli mixture into the terrine mold. Put the terrine in a larger baking pan half full with hot water and bake for 10 minutes. We call this a "bain-marie."

Green Beans with Parsley
HARICOTS VERTS À LA MAÎTRE D'HÔTEL

This is a very useful dish, because it can be served with a lamb roast, an omelet, fried fish, or almost any entrée.

SERVES 4

2 pounds fresh green beans

½ cup fresh or canned chicken broth

2 tablespoons butter

Half a lemon, juiced

1 tablespoon flour

4 tablespoons chopped fresh parsley

Salt and pepper

1 Cook the beans in salted boiled water for about 10 minutes or until tender. Drain.

2 In a skillet, bring the chicken broth to a simmer and add the butter and lemon juice. Then gradually stir in the flour.

3 Add the beans, parsley, salt and pepper. Stir and simmer for a few minutes.

NOTE You can use frozen green beans which cook more quickly. You can also use a chicken boullion cube dissolved in boiling water for the chicken broth.

Baked Zucchini
GRATIN DE COURGETTES

SERVES 4

*Except for the Béchamel Sauce, this is simplicity itself —
a great dish.*

> 2 pounds zucchini
> 1 tablespoon butter
> Pinch pepper
> 2 cups Béchamel Sauce (see page 109)
> 2 cups grated Swiss cheese

1 Preheat the oven to 450 °F.

2 Trim and cut the zucchini into 1/2-inch slices.

3 Boil the zucchini in salted water for 5 minutes or less.
Drain.

4 Grease an 8 × 8-inch baking dish with butter. Then
Arrange the zucchini on the bottom. Sprinkle the zucchini with pepper.

5 Make the Béchamel Sauce.

6 Cover the zucchini with the sauce.

7 Sprinkle with cheese and bake for 20 minutes.

Ratatouille

1 large eggplant

5 zucchini

1 red pepper, diced

6 tomatoes, diced

1 chopped onion

3 garlic cloves, chopped

3 tablespoons olive oil

1 ½ teaspoon salt

½ teaspoon pepper

1 Trim and dice unpeeled eggplant into 1/2-inch cubes.

2 Trim zucchini and cut lengthwise in half, then each half into 1-inch pieces.

3 In a large skillet sauté onion and garlic in olive oil for 5 minutes.

4 Add eggplant, zucchini, red pepper, cover and cook for 15 minutes over medium heat.

5 Add tomatoes, salt, and pepper. Cook uncovered over low heat for 40 minutes, stirring from time to time.

6 Serve hot or cold.

Artichoke Stew

RAGOÛT D'ARTICHAUTS

SERVES 4

If you like artichokes, I guarantee you will like this dish. It will be a surprise to most Americans who, I believe, have never done artichokes this way.

8 artichokes

½ lemon

4 garlic cloves, chopped

4 tablespoons chopped fresh parsley

3 tablespoons olive oil

1 onion, chopped

6 red potatoes, peeled and cut in half

1 bay leaf

1 teaspoon dried thyme

1 teaspoon salt

¼ teaspoon pepper

2 cups water

1   Cut the stems from the artichokes and trim the base of each one so they will lie flat. Using your hands, snap off the green, stiff leaves until you reach the soft, light green leaves. Cut off the soft cone of leaves, leaving only the choke behind. Trim any dark green parts. Scrape out the fuzz and small leaves from inside each artichoke bottom, then rub each one with lemon. Set the artichoke hearts aside.

2   Combine the garlic with the parsley. Set aside.

3   In a heavy skillet, heat the oil and sauté the onion for about 5 minutes or until light brown.

4   In the same skillet, place the artichoke hearts round side up. Then stuff each one with the garlic and parsley mixture.

5   Arrange the potatoes on top, add the bay leaf, thyme, salt, pepper, and water. Cover and cook over medium heat for 30 minutes.

6   Discard the bay leaf before serving.

Sauces

Tomato Sauce
SAUCE TOMATE

MAKES
ABOUT 4 CUPS

This is a very simple tomato sauce, but one of the best I have ever encountered, simple—but right on the button.

2 tablespoons olive oil
1 onion, chopped
4 garlic cloves, chopped
2 tablespoons tomato paste
8 ripe tomatoes, chopped
1 teaspoon dried thyme
1 bay leaf
1 teaspoon sugar
2 cups canned or fresh chicken broth
1 teaspoon salt
¼ teaspoon pepper

1 In a skillet, heat the oil, then sauté the onion and garlic.

2 Lower the heat and add the tomato paste, tomatoes, thyme, bay leaf, sugar, chicken broth, salt, and pepper. Cover and simmer over low heat for about 30 minutes, stirring occasionally.

3 Remove the bay leaf and purée the sauce in a food processor. If you want a smoother sauce, strain it through a fine sieve.

Béchamel Sauce

SAUCE BÉCHAMEL

This is a cream sauce with nutmeg added for fragrance and depth of taste. I call it a basic sauce because it is used so frequently.

MAKES
ABOUT 2 CUPS

 2 tablespoons butter
 ¼ cup flour, sifted
 2 cups milk
 Pinch ground nutmeg
 Salt and pepper

1 Melt the butter in a heavy saucepan over very low heat.

2 Stir the flour into the butter.

3 Pour in the milk and whisk constantly until all the lumps are smoothed out.

4 Add the nutmeg, season with salt and pepper, and simmer uncovered for 15 to 20 minutes over very low heat, stirring often.

5 The sauce is ready when it is thick and smooth.

Hollandaise Sauce
SAUCE HOLLANDAISE

**MAKES
ABOUT 2 CUPS**

This is a very rich sauce, crammed with butter, that is succulent over steamed broccoli or asparagus.

3 egg yolks
1 tablespoon lemon juice
2 tablespoons water
½ teaspoon salt
Pinch pepper
½ pound butter in small pieces

1 In a heatproof mixing bowl, combine the egg yolks, lemon juice, water, salt and pepper.

2 Place the same bowl in a roasting pan half filled with simmering water and cook over low heat. We call this process "bain-marie."

3 Gradually add the butter pieces to the mixing bowl and whisk constantly until the sauce begins to thicken.

4 Adjust the seasoning if needed.

NOTE: You can save the egg whites in the refrigerator, covered, for macaroons or meringues.

Shallots and Red Wine Sauce
SAUCE BORDELAISE

This is a dieter's delight, with very little fat. It's an interesting sauce — very good over a pot roast.

MAKES ABOUT 2 CUPS

> 2 tablespoons butter
> 6 shallots, minced
> 1 cup red wine (Burgundy or Cabernet)
> 1 teaspoon flour
> 1 cup fresh or canned chicken broth
> 1 bay leaf
> ½ teaspoon dried thyme
> ½ teaspoon salt
> Pinch pepper
> 1 tablespoon sour cream

1 Melt the butter in a saucepan and sauté the shallots over medium heat for about 5 minutes or until softened and lightly brown.

2 Add the wine and simmer uncovered for 5 minutes over low heat.

3 Lower the heat and add the flour, chicken broth, bay leaf, thyme, salt, and pepper. Cover and simmer for about 30 minutes over very low heat.

4 Discard the bay leaf, stir in the sour cream, and serve.

Béarnaise Sauce
SAUCE BÉARNAISE

MAKES
ABOUT 2 CUPS

This is slightly less rich than the Hollandaise Sauce. The richness here is tempered with the white wine and red wine vinegar. The tarragon adds its own freshness to the sauce.

2 shallots, minced

½ cup dry white wine

½ cup red wine vinegar

Salt and pepper

3 egg yolks

½ pound butter, cut in small pieces

2 tablespoons chopped fresh tarragon

1. Combine the shallots, wine, vinegar, salt, and pepper in a small saucepan and boil over medium heat for about 15 minutes or until the liquid is reduced by half.

2. Remove the saucepan from the heat and let it cool a few minutes.

3. In the same saucepan, add the egg yolks one by one and stir gently.

4. Return the saucepan, to very low heat. Add the butter slowly, whisking constantly.

5. Whisk in the tarragon. Keep whisking for a few minutes until the sauce becomes thicker and creamier.

Spicy Provençal Sauce
ROUILLE

**MAKES
ABOUT 1 CUP**

This is very good spread on toasted slices of a baguette.

1 slice sandwich bread
½ cup milk
4 garlic cloves
1 chile pepper
1 egg yolk
⅔ cup olive oil
Salt and pepper

1. Soak the bread in the milk.

2. In a mortar and pestle, crush the garlic cloves until the mixture is smooth.

3. Seed and chop the chile pepper. Then add it to the garlic in the mortar and make a homogenized paste.

4. Squeeze the bread between your hands and discard the milk.

5. Put the garlic, chile pepper, and softened bread into a processor and blend the mixture.

6. Add the egg yolk and blend once more.

7. Gradually add the oil, drop by drop at first, then in a thin stream once the sauce begins to thicken. The sauce is ready when thick. Adjust the seasoning with salt and pepper.

NOTE: If you want to increase the spiciness of the sauce, add another chile pepper. You could use a processor instead of a mortar and pestle. Simply keep adding ingredients to the processor.

Mayonnaise
SAUCE MAYONNAISE

MAKES
ABOUT 1 CUP

There is nothing like homemade mayonnaise. It can make the difference between an ordinary sandwich and a great one.

> 1 egg yolk
> 1 tablespoon extra strong Dijon mustard
> ½ teaspoon salt
> Pinch pepper
> 1 cup vegetable oil

1 In a mixing bowl, combine the egg yolk, mustard, salt, and pepper.

2 Using an electric blender on very low speed, gradually add the oil to the bowl, drop by drop at first, then in a thin stream once it begins to thicken.

3 The mayonnaise is ready when it becomes thick.

Desserts

Lemon Meringue Pie
TARTE AU CITRON MERINGUÉE

SERVES
4 TO 6

If you have the time, make your own pie crust. If not, buy a ready-made one at the grocery store.

> 1 pie crust
> 2 lemons
> 3 eggs
> 1 cup sugar
> ¼ pound butter, in small pieces
> ½ cup egg whites

1 Preheat the oven to 400 °F.

2 Keep the crust pastry in its aluminum tin and prick the crust with a fork to prevent it from puffing up.

3 Bake the crust 15 minutes or until light brown. Set aside. Keep the oven hot.

4 Grate the lemons, using only the yellow outer skin. Stop grating once you reach white pith beneath. Using the same lemons, juice them. In a mixing bowl, combine the eggs, lemon juice, lemon peel, 1/2 cup sugar, and butter. Whisk together.

5 Fill the crust with the filling.

6 Bake the pie for 40 minutes. Keep the oven hot.

7 Meanwhile, make the meringue. In a mixing bowl whisk the egg whites and the remaining 1/2 cup sugar until stiff peaks form, stirring constantly until the mixture is smooth.

8 Spread the meringue over the pie, in whatever swirls you like.

9 Bake the pie 8–10 minutes or until the meringue gets lightly brown.

10 Serve cold.

Raspberry Pie
TARTE AUX FRAMBOISES

SERVES
4 TO 6

This is a very simple dessert to put together — yet, very elegant in presentation. Serve Chantilly (see page 121) and vanilla ice cream with it.

1 ready-made pie crust
10 ounces fresh raspberries
8 tablespoons raspberry jelly

1 Preheat the oven to 400 °F.

2 Keeping the pastry in its tin plate, prick it with a fork to prevent it from puffing up.

3 Bake the crust for about 25 minutes or until light brown.

4 Cool the crust and arrange the raspberries over the top.

5 Spread the jelly over the raspberries. If the jelly is too thick to spread easily, dilute it with a bit of boiling water.

Chantilly

1 cup heavy whipping cream, chilled
2 tablespoons sugar
Few drops vanilla extract (optional)

**MAKES
ABOUT 2 CUPS**

1 Using an electric beater at low speed, whisk the cream until foamy.

2 Once the cream begins to thicken, add the sugar and the vanilla.

3 Increase the speed to medium and continue beating for a few seconds until peaks form.

Apple Tart
TARTE TATIN

The puff pastry used here is a great idea, better than a regular crust. Also, the golden delicious apples are a delicacy — sweet and intensely fragrant.

> 1 frozen puff pastry sheet
> ⅔ cup sugar
> 6 tablespoons water
> ¼ pound butter, in small pieces
> 5 golden delicious apples
> Whipping cream

1 Preheat the oven to 450 °F.

2 Take the pastry out of the freezer.

3 Combine the sugar and water in a 9-inch round cake pan and cook over the stove for 5 minutes or until sugar turns color and becomes caramelized.

4 At this point, sprinkle the butter pieces over the sugar and stir thoroughly. Remove from the heat.

5 Peel, halve, and core the apples. Cut each half into 4 pieces.

6 Arrange the apples on top of the caramel in a pretty design and cook 2 minutes over medium heat.

8 Place the cake pan in the oven and bake for 20 minutes.

9 Take the cake pan from the oven and unroll the puff pastry on top of the apples. Turn down the edges of the puff pastry inside the cake pan.

10 Put the cake pan back in the oven and bake for 30 more minutes.

11 Turn the cake pan upside down so that the turnover has the apples face up with the puff pastry on the bottom. Serve warm with whipping cream in a pitcher on the side.

Chocolate Cake

GÂTEAU AU CHOCOLAT

SERVES
6 TO 8

This is a basically a chocolate sponge cake, made somewhat richer by the butter which is melted with the chocolate chips. A blackberry sorbet would be good with this, or an orange sherbet.

> 12 ounces semi-sweet chocolate chips
> ¼ pound butter
> 1 cup sugar
> 8 eggs, separated
> 7 tablespoons sifted flour, divided
> Powdered sugar (optional)

1   Preheat the oven to 400 °F.

2   Place a roasting pan filled half way with boiling water on the stove. Place a heat-resistant bowl in the center of the roasting pan.

3   In the bowl, combine the chocolate chips with butter over low heat, stirring constantly until the chocolate is melted. Set aside.

4   In a separate bowl, beat the sugar with the egg yolks until the mixture turns pale yellow.

5   In another mixing bowl, beat the egg whites until peaks form.

6 Pour the chocolate mixture into the egg yolk mixture and stir.

7 Delicately fold the egg whites into the chocolate mixture.

8 Add 6 tablespoons of the flour and mix gently until combined.

9 Butter a 9-inch round cake pan and use the remaining 1 tablespoon of flour to dust it. Shake off any excess. Pour the cake into the pan.

10 Bake the cake for 35 minutes. Cool before serving.

11 If you wish, you can decorate the top with powdered sugar. If you want a pattern, put a paper doily down on top of the cake and sieve the powdered sugar over the cake.

Raspberry and **Almond Cake**

GÂTEAU AUX FRAMBOISES ET AMANDES

SERVES 6

This is quite an elaborate two-layer cake with fresh raspberries, glazed with currant jelly, filled with whipped cream, and as a final touch, adorned with ground almonds.

3 eggs, separated
1 cup granulated sugar, divided
½ lemon, juiced
½ cup semolina
2 tablespoons ground almonds
Butter to grease cake pan
Flour to flour cake pan
2 tablespoons red currant jelly
1 teaspoon water
1 cup whipping cream, divided
6 ounces fresh raspberries
½ cup chopped almonds

1 Preheat the oven to 350 °F.

2 Whisk the egg whites until stiff peaks form. Set aside.

3 In a separate bowl, whisk the egg yolks with 1/2 cup of the sugar and lemon juice.

4 Add the semolina and 2 tablespoons of the ground almonds.

5 Delicately fold the egg whites into the egg yolk mixture.

Do so until no more white is seen in the yellow mixture.

6 Butter and flour an 8-inch round cake pan. Turn the cake mixture into the pan and bake it for 25 minutes. Let it cool for 5 minutes, then unmold on a rack. Cut the cake horizontally into 2 equal layers and let cool.

7 In a small saucepan, melt the currant jelly with the water over medium heat. Let it cool.

8 Using an electric beater first at low speed, whisk the cream until foamy. Then increase the speed to medium and add the remaining sugar. Continue beating for a few seconds until peaks form. Set aside.

9 Place the first layer of cake on a serving plate and cover with 3/4 cup of the whipping cream. Next, place the second layer and arrange the raspberries on top, leaving an inch of the perimeter of the cake clear.

10 Using a pastry brush, glaze the raspberries and side of the cake with the jelly, leaving 1 inch clear on the perimeter.

11 Cover the sides of the cake with the chopped almonds.

12 Spoon the remaining whipped cream into a pastry bag fitted with a medium star tip. Add a border of whipping cream around the 1 inch clear space on the perimeter of the cake as a final decoration.

Raspberry Sauce
COULIS DE FRAMBOISE

**MAKES
ABOUT 1 CUP**

This would be good over tapioca pudding or custard, or bread pudding for that matter.

12 ounces fresh or frozen raspberries

½ cup sugar

1 If necessary, defrost the raspberries. If there is any juice, discard it.

2 Place the raspberries and sugar in a food processor and blend until the sugar is completely dissolved.

3 Strain through a fine sieve. Discard the seeds.

Pears with **Ice Cream** and **Chocolate Sauce**

POIRES BELLE HELENE

Divine decadence!

SERVES 4

 4 pears
 6 tablespoons sugar, divided
 1 cup water
 6 ounces semi-sweet chocolate chips
 1 egg yolk
 1 pint vanilla ice cream

1 Peel, halve, and core the pears.

2 In a saucepan combine the pears with 4 tablespoons sugar and the water. Cover and simmer over low heat for 15 minutes.

3 Fill a roasting pan half way with boiling water and place on the stove. Place a heat resistant bowl in the center of the roasting pan.

4 In the bowl put the chocolate chips, egg yolk, and the remaining sugar. Cook over very low heat until the chocolate is melted. Stir the mixture constantly.

5 Drain the pears.

6 On each individual plate, place 2 pear halves. Top them with 2 scoops of ice cream. Pour the hot chocolate sauce on the top. Serve immediately.

Cherry Pudding
CLAFOUTIS AUX CERISES

SERVES
6 TO 8

Butter to grease the pie pan
1 ½ pounds fresh bing cherries, stems removed
4 eggs
1 cup half-and-half
½ cup sugar
½ cup flour
1 tablespoon powdered sugar

1 Preheat the oven to 400 °F.

2 Generously grease a 9-inch pie pan with butter. Then arrange the cherries on the bottom of the pan.

3 In a large mixing bowl, combine the eggs, half-and-half, and sugar.

4 Sift the flour over the eggs and sugar, and mix well.

5 Pour the batter over the cherries and bake for 1 hour.

6 When the cherry pudding is still warm, sprinkle it with powered sugar.

7 Serve warm or cold.

Vanilla Custard
CRÈME ANGLAISE

I like this with chocolate cake served alongside.

**MAKES
ABOUT 2 CUPS**

    2 cups milk
    2 vanilla beans
    6 egg yolks
    ½ cup sugar

1   Combine the milk and vanilla beans in a saucepan, bring to a simmer, and then turn off the heat.

2   In a large mixing bowl, whisk the egg yolks with the sugar.

3   Delicately pour the milk and vanilla beans into the egg yolk mixture and whisk until thoroughly combined.

4   Return this mixture to the saucepan and simmer over very low heat for about 20 minutes. Stir very often until the custard turns thick and coats the back of the spoon. Do not overcook.

5   Discard the vanilla beans and strain the custard through a fine sieve.

6   Cool before serving.

Crème Brûlée

This is absurdly simple, but marvelous just the same.

4 eggs yolks
¼ cup sugar, divided
2 cups heavy whipping cream
½ teaspoon vanilla extract, alcohol free

1 Preheat the oven to 300 °F.

2 In a small mixing bowl, beat the egg yolks well with 1 tablespoon of sugar. Set aside.

3 Heat the whipping cream in a double-boiler or "bainmarie" over medium heat. Slowly stir the egg yolk mixture into the cream.

4 Turn off the heat, add the vanilla, and mix.

5 Pour the custard into 4 individual ramekins or custard cups.

6 Place the ramekins in a deep roasting pan in a doubleboiler. Bake for 40 minutes.

7 Remove the ramekins from the roasting pan and chill for 1 hour.

8 Sprinkle the remaining sugar over each chilled ramekin.

9 Broil the custard in the ramekins for 3 to 5 minutes in the oven until the sugar becomes caramelized.

10 Chill for at least 1 hour before serving.

Custard with **Caramel Topping**

FLAN AU CARAMEL

SERVES
6 TO 8

This is somewhat richer than Crème Brûlée — more eggs, more egg yolks.

1 ½ cups sugar, divided

3 tablespoons water

4 cups milk

1 vanilla bean

6 eggs

6 egg yolks

1 Preheat the oven to 450 °F.

2 To make the caramel, in a small pan, combine 1/2 cup of sugar with the water and boil over high heat for about 5 minutes or until dark brown. Immediately pour the caramel into a heatproof flan dish. Set aside.

3 In a separate pan, bring the milk with the vanilla bean to a boil. Take off the stove.

4 In a large mixing bowl, whisk the whole eggs and yolks with the remaining 1 cup of sugar. Stir in the hot milk and discard the vanilla bean.

5 Strain the custard through a fine sieve to dissolve any small lumps.

6 Pour the custard into the flan dish in which you have already poured the caramel. Place the flan dish in a deep roasting pan in a double-boiler or "bain-marie."

7 Bake the custard for 45 minutes.

8 Wait until the custard is cold to unmold it. Serve it cold.

Floating Islands
ILES FLOTTANTES

SERVES 4

This is a beautiful dish in presentation. Both adults and children love it.

> 1 vanilla bean
> 4 cups milk
> 6 eggs, separated
> 1 ¾ cups sugar, divided
> 4 tablespoons water

1 Add the vanilla bean to the milk in a saucepan, bring to a simmer, and then turn off the heat.

2 In a large mixing bowl, whisk the egg yolks with 1 cup sugar.

3 Delicately pour the milk and vanilla bean into the egg yolk mixture and whisk thoroughly.

4 Return the custard to the saucepan, and simmer over very low heat for about 20 minutes, stirring very often, until the custard turns thick and coats the back of the spoon. Do not overcook it.

5 Discard the vanilla bean and strain the custard through a fine sieve. Cool.

6 Fill a large pan with water and bring it to a simmer.

7 Beat the egg whites until stiff, then add 1/2 cup of sugar. Beat until peaks are formed.

8 Use a tablespoon to scoop out the spoonfuls of the "islands" and drop into the simmering water. Each island should be the size of a potato. Poach each island 30 seconds on each side. Drain the islands on a flat surface and repeat the operation until you empty the bowl.

9 To make the caramel, combine the remaining 1/4 cup sugar with 4 tablespoons of water in a small saucepan, and cook over high heat for about 4 minutes or until the caramel turns dark brown. Immediately pour it over the islands.

10 Carefully pour the custard into a serving bowl, place the islands on top, and chill before serving.

Chocolate Mousse
MOUSSE AU CHOCOLAT

SERVES 6

The orange juice makes a difference here. I think you will like it.

6 ounces semi-sweet dark chocolate chips
2 tablespoons butter
1 tablespoon fresh orange juice
3 egg yolks
2 tablespoons sugar
5 egg whites

1   Fill a roasting pan half way with water and place on the stove. Place a heat resistant bowl in the center of the roasting pan.

2   In the bowl, combine the chocolate chips, butter, and orange juice, and cook over medium heat, stirring constantly until the chocolate is melted. Then turn off the heat.

3   Stir the egg yolks and sugar into the chocolate mixture.

4   In a separate mixing bowl, beat the egg whites until stiff peaks form.

5   Gently fold the egg whites into the chocolate mixture. Be careful not to overwork this process—if you do, the mousse will lose volume. At this point you shouldn't see any white left in the chocolate mixture.

6   Pour into a large serving bowl or ramekins and chill for at least 2 hours.

Chocolate Truffles

These make an exceptional holiday gift. You can use shredded coconut in instead of cocoa for a different look and taste. Pick a pretty tin for these delights.

8 ounces unsweetened chocolate bars, in small pieces
2 tablespoons fresh orange juice
1 stick butter, in small pieces
1 cup powdered sugar
2 tablespoons unsweetened cocoa

1   Place a roasting pan filled half way with water on the stove. Place a heat resistant bowl in the center of the pan.

2   In the bowl, combine the broken chocolate bars with the orange juice and butter and cook over medium heat until the chocolate is melted. Remove the bowl from the heat.

3   Stir in the sugar until thoroughly combined.

4   Chill the bowl for 2 hours.

5   Spread the cocoa on a plate.

6   Use a teaspoon to break off pieces of the chilled chocolate mixture, and roll them between your palms into balls the size of large olives.

7   Delicately roll each truffle into cocoa powder.

8   Store in a cool place.

Caramel Syrup
SAUCE CARAMEL

MAKES
ABOUT 1 CUP

This is excellent over vanilla ice cream, or over a sponge cake, or perhaps over the two together.

1 cup sugar
½ cup water
4 tablespoons sour cream
3 tablespoons butter, in small pieces

1 Combine the sugar with the water in a saucepan and cook over high heat for about 10 minutes or until brown.

2 Remove the saucepan from the heat and mix the sour cream into the sugar-water mixture.

3 Add the butter and stir until thoroughly combined.

4 Serve hot or cold.

Index

Books by The Crossing Press

Bill Taylor Cooks Chicken
By Bill Taylor

As the former Corporate Chef at The Crossing Press, Bill Taylor has prepared hundreds of chicken dishes and has chosen the very best for this book.

$12.95 • Paper • ISBN 1-58091-045-9

Everyday Tofu: From Pancakes to Pizza
By Gary Landgrebe

This book offers all Americans an opportunity to incorporate tofu into their everyday diets. We are not asking them to change their habits. We say sincerely that Americans who have remained aloof from the tofu craze will honestly be pleased by these recipes which combine tofu with their favorite foods and seasonings to create Western style main dishes, breads, and desserts.

$12.95 • Paper • ISBN 1-58091-047-5

The Great Barbecue Companion
By Bruce Bjorkman

A collection of sauces covering the best barbecue flavors: sweet, savory, hot, and spicy — sometimes mixing all four. A mouth-watering array of recipes...add this one to your library.—National Barbecue News

$12.95 • Paper • ISBN 0-89594-806-0

Innovative Soy Cooking
By Trudie Burnham

This collection of recipes is perhaps the most original kitchen work that has crossed our Editor's desk in a long time. Here are tofu, tempeh and miso dishes we drooled over!

$6.95 • Paper • ISBN 0-89594-962-8

BOOKS BY THE CROSSING PRESS

International Vegetarian Cooking

By Judy Ridgway

This collection of more than 400 new vegetarian dishes was adapted from the world's most popular cuisines. Includes dietary guidelines, menu planning tips and time-saving suggestions.

$14.95 • Paper • ISBN 0-89594-854-0

Japanese Vegetarian Cooking

By Patricia Richfield

Easy-to-follow directions, information on techniques, plus a glossary of Japanese ingredients make this a must-have cookbook for all Japanese food fans.

$14.95 • Paper • ISBN 0-89594-805-2

Jerk: Barbecue from Jamaica

By Helen Willinsky

An inspired collection of fiery recipes from the Caribbean islands written by an expert on the topic.—Gourmet Retailer,

After reading her descriptions I wanted to grab my passport and catch a plane.—Chile Pepper

$12.95 • Paper • ISBN 0-89594-439-1

Low-Fat Vegetarian Cooking

By Sue Kreitzman

Adapting vegetarian dishes from the cuisines of the world, Kreitzman has created new low-fat or non-fat dishes for vegetarians and anyone wanting to reduce the fat in their diets.

$14.95 • Paper • ISBN 0-89594-834-6

Books by The Crossing Press

Marinades: Dry Rubs, Pastes & Marinades for Poultry, Meat, Seafood, Cheese & Vegetables

By Jim Tarantino

The most comprehensive book available! Tarantino recreates marinades and flavoring pastes from all over the world, and provides instructions for preparing seafood, poultry, meat, vegetables, and cheese-indoors and out.

$16.95 • Paper • ISBN 0-89594-531-2

Noodle Fusion: Asian Pasta Dishes for Western Palates

By Andrea Chesman and Dorothy Rankin

This book has it all: from spring rolls to egg rolls, wontons to pot stickers; from cool salads to comforting soups; from vegetarian delights to deep sea wonders; from chicken and duck, to beef and pork exotica. Included is a clear description of the various Asian noodles, both fresh and dried, which are available in their astonishing array at most supermarkets.

$16.95 • Paper • ISBN 0-89594-956-3

Salad Dressings

By Teresa H. Burns

This little book is full of creative dressings that are fresh, healthy and delicious.

$6.95 • Paper • ISBN 0-89594-895-8

Sauces for Pasta!

By K. Trabant with A. Chesman

This little book has my favorite new and old sauces.—Grace Kirschenbaum, World of Cookbooks

$8.95 • Paper • ISBN 0-89594-403-0

BOOKS BY THE CROSSING PRESS

Secrets of a Jewish Baker, 1994 James Beard award winner

By George Greenstein

... Greenstein's book is easily worth several times its price.
—Vogue

$16.95 • Paper • ISBN 0-89594-605-X

The Spice Box

By Manju Shivraj Singh

An imaginative collection of recipes that will be of interest to the seasoned chef of Indian cuisine. A cookbook well suited to the adventurous vegetarian.—Publishers Weekly

$12.95 • Paper • ISBN 0-89594-053-1

Truffles, Candies, and Confections

By Carole Bloom

...Bloom has the rare ability to clearly explain technical procedures and write a recipe that's easy to follow.—Los Angeles Times

$14.95 • Paper • ISBN 0-89594-833-8

To receive a current catalog from The Crossing Press
please call toll-free, 800-777-1048.
Visit our Web site: **www.crossingpress.com**